40p

The Ethics of Paul

GW00808909

Colin Hart

Lecturer in Practical Theology, St John's College, Nottingham

GROVE BOOKS LIMITED
RIDLEY HALL RD CAMBRIDGE CB3 9HU

Contents

Acknowledgments

I am grateful to Rev Greg Forster and Dr Dave Leal, fellow-members of the Grove Ethics Group, for their comments on an early draft of this booklet.

For the purpose of this booklet—the third in a series of four—I will concentrate on the epistles which were almost certainly written by the Apostle Paul himself—Romans, 1 and 2 Corinthians, Galatians, Philippians, 1 and 2 Thessalonians (some commentators do not think Paul wrote 2 Thessalonians, but it does not belong with Ephesians or the pastoral epistles). Philemon, Colossians, Ephesians, 1 and 2 Timothy and Titus, which may have been written either by Paul himself later in his life or by one of his followers, will be the subject of the fourth booklet. Dividing the Pauline literature between two booklets in this way acknowledges the important differences in outlook between the two groups of epistles, but does not imply any particular view about authorship.

The Cover Illustration is by Peter Ashton

First Impression October 1999
ISSN 0951-2659
ISBN 1 85174 416 9

1
Introduction

The Nature of Paul's Ethical Teaching

Over thirty years ago, the author of a valuable study on Pauline ethics (Furnish, 1968) gave what remains an accurate summary, despite the subsequent significant changes in scholarly approaches to Paul's theology (p 212):

> The study of the Pauline ethic ... is not the study of his ethical theory, for he had none, nor of his code for Christian living, for he gave none. It is the study, first of all, of the theological convictions which underlie Paul's concrete exhortations and instructions, and, secondly, of the way those convictions shape his responses to practical questions of conduct.

As Furnish suggests, Paul never sets out his ethical thinking systematically or comprehensively; rather, his ethical teaching seems to have been devised in response to specific situations and problems in the churches he addressed.

Paul's ethical teaching falls naturally into three categories, which may be termed 'Ethical Motivation,' 'Sources, Methods and Guiding Principles' and 'Teaching on Specific Subjects.' I will follow this threefold division in this booklet in such a way that the proportions of the sections correspond roughly to their relative prominence in Paul's own writing.

Understanding Paul's Ethical Teaching

Even with regard to the subjects Paul does discuss in his surviving epistles, the occasional nature of the literature can make it difficult to be sure what he is saying because only one side of the dialogue has survived. To use a common analogy, reading Paul's epistles can be like overhearing one end of a telephone conversation: at some points it is fairly obvious what the other party has said, but in other places it is quite obscure. Frör (1995) is a recent attempt to fill in this historical background by composing letters which Paul might have received from various members of the church in Corinth.

As Richard Hays (1996, p 16) has pointed out, there are also other crucial gaps in the information required for reliable interpretation:

> How had Paul preached the gospel to them originally? What norms of behaviour had he already sought to inculcate? What shared assumptions were so fundamental that they remained implicit rather than explicit in Paul's correspondence?

A good example of this lack of clarity occurs in 1 Corinthians 6.12, 13, where Paul is criticizing his readers for their lax attitude to matters of sexual morality. Most modern English translations use quotation marks to indicate that Paul appears to be citing slogans favoured by the Corinthians themselves—probably excerpts from their letter to him which he is answering. However, quotation marks did not exist when the original manuscripts were written and their insertion is therefore a matter of editorial judgment.

It does seem likely that the slogan, 'All things are lawful for me,' which occurs twice in verse 12 (and also in 10.23), was a maxim frequently cited by the Corinthians. However, it is impossible to be sure whether it originated with them or if they were quoting from some other source—perhaps even Paul himself. In the following verse, 'Food is meant for the stomach and the stomach for food,' is probably being quoted from the Corinthians, and 'The body is not meant for immorality but for the Lord, and the Lord for the body,' is almost certainly Paul's own comment, but it is unclear whether the intervening words—'and God will destroy both one and the other'—are part of the quotation or part of Paul's response.

Some of Paul's letters—especially Galatians—are written to oppose the doctrines of other Christian teachers whom he considered to be gravely mistaken. Regrettably, our only source today in seeking what those 'false teachers' actually taught is Paul's denunciations of them, but he was not necessarily trying to be fair to them or to present their ministry and message in the best possible light. Galatians 6.12, 13, for example, in which he attributes scurrilous motives to his opponents, is an insult, not a factual statement.

Development or Influence of Circumstances?

Further uncertainty about interpretation concerns the possibility that Paul's thinking may have developed during his career. In particular, some writers have suggested that Paul's ethical thinking changed when he came to realize that Christ's second coming was not as imminent as he had supposed. To some extent, judgments on development are circular, since the presence in an epistle of opinions or attitudes judged to be characteristic of Paul's early or late writings may be used as evidence for dating the epistle.

The alternative to this theory is that Paul's approach was influenced by the situation which he was addressing. If he stressed certain aspects of a complex truth which he felt his readers were neglecting while underemphasizing those things he considered they understood only too well, then the implied setting of the epistle must be taken into account and comparisons should be made between different documents. Furthermore, Paul may have employed terms he knew his readers would have found congenial and for strategic reasons he may have agreed with them everywhere he could.

The New Approach to Pauline Theology

In the last twenty years or so, many scholars have accepted a radically new approach to the interpretation of Paul's theology. They have been convinced by E P Sanders's rejection of the traditional 'Lutheran' view that the central message of Romans and Galatians is the question how human beings can be accepted, or acquitted, by God.

According to the traditional view, Judaism taught that the way to salvation was by performing good deeds in obedience to the Old Testament law. But Paul repudiates this approach and asserts that the only basis on which anyone can approach God is by trusting in his promise and in the saving work of Christ. Sanders suggests that the subject of both epistles is actually the admission of Gentiles into membership of the people of God. Of the commentaries on Romans referred to in this booklet, Cranfield and Moo broadly represent the traditional interpretation of the epistle, whereas Dunn and Ziesler are influenced by Sanders.

2

Ethical Motivation

The Allegation of Antinomianism

One of the most frequent allegations made against Paul was that he taught and practised antinomianism (abolishing all moral rules and norms) or that it was an inescapable logical corollary of his gospel of grace and freedom. This allegation is expressed in three forms in the epistle to the Romans, as Paul imagines his opponents accusing him of saying, 'Let us do evil, that good may come' (3.8), 'Let us persevere in sin, that grace may abound' (6.1) and 'Let us sin because we are not under law but under grace' (6.15).

Paul not only repudiates the allegation with a strong expression rendered variously as 'By no means!,' 'God forbid!,' 'Certainly not!' and 'No way!' but also explains that the various metaphors which he uses to expound his message of salvation by grace all naturally have ethical implications.

The Imperative in the Indicative

Paul's fundamental ethical teaching can be expressed in the slogan 'The imperative in the indicative' or, more simply, 'Become what you are.' In other words, the facts about God's action in Christ and believers' experience of new life (the 'indicative') carry with them certain implications about behaviour (the 'imperative'); Paul's ethical exhortations consist of urging his readers to put those implications into practice. This argument can be seen simply in 1 Corinthians 5.7,

> Cleanse out the old leaven, that you may be a new batch, as you are unleavened, for Christ, our Passover lamb, has been sacrificed.

The annual practice in Judaism of removing all trace of fermented dough from the house before the Passover festival is here being used to symbolize the removal of evil influences, a symbolic interpretation which was quite common in Jewish thought of that period. Paul is telling his readers that because in principle they have been purified from evil influences, they must also ensure that they are purified in practice. He then extends the metaphor, explaining that this purification occurred by means of the death of Jesus, interpreted as the sacrifice of a Passover lamb.

Therefore

This fundamental connection between the indicative and the imperative in Paul's teaching is sometimes expressed in English translations by the adverb 'therefore.' The clearest example occurs in Romans 12.1,

> I beseech you therefore, brothers [and sisters], through the mercies of God, to present your bodies as a living sacrifice, holy and pleasing to God, which is your rational worship.

Most commentators interpret this exhortation as referring back to the whole argument of the preceding eleven chapters, in which the apostle has not only explained the experience of salvation in Christ which his readers are enjoying, but has also set it in the context of God's mysterious plan for the salvation of the world. The significance of this verse in Paul's ethical teaching is shown by Matera's judgment (1996, p 206) that

> More than any other Pauline letter, [Romans] challenges believers to frame ethics within the horizon of worship and thanksgiving, so that the moral life will become the total giving of oneself within the context of a believing community for the praise and glory of God.

But not all occurrences of the word 'therefore' are as clear as this. A characteristic of the Greek of the New Testament, by comparison with English, is that Greek almost always joins sentences together by means of a conjunction or particle, such as 'for,' 'but' or 'therefore,' even in cases where the connection is quite weak. In English a link is made explicit only if the author considers it to be important. In many cases, the correct way to render a paragraph of the Greek New Testament into idiomatic English is to ignore those weak connecting words.

Commentators and translators may legitimately disagree with one another as to whether particular occurrences of the word 'therefore' are theologically significant or do not need to be translated. 1 Thessalonians 4.1 is an example of this uncertainty: the Authorized Version translated the particle as 'then,' but most modern translations omit it altogether, whereas both Rosner (1995) and Schrage (1988) cite the verse as an example of the use of 'therefore' expressing the relationship between the indicative and the imperative.

Despite this linguistic ambiguity, Paul certainly tends to put the hortatory and ethical material towards the end of his epistles as the corollary of the theological assertions of the earlier chapters.

What God has Done for the Believer in Christ

One of Paul's main ways to describe what God has achieved in Christ is by means of the verb *dikaioō* (translated as 'acquit' or 'make righteous') and the abstract noun *dikaiosyne* (translated as 'justification' or 'righteousness'). The interpretation of the meaning of these words has constituted a major difference between Catholic and Protestant interpreters of Pauline theology.

As Ziesler (1972, p 1) asks, 'First, does *dikaioō* mean "declare righteous" or "make righteous"? Second, does the noun *dikaiosyne* refer to a relationship, or a way of living, or both?' On the basis of the Hebrew and Greek background of the words, and of study of relevant passages from Romans and Galatians, he concludes that justification and righteousness belong together and should not be separated. In particular, he argues (p 1)

> that the verb 'justify' is used relationally, often with the forensic meaning 'acquit,' but that the noun, and the adjective *dikaios*, have behavioural meanings, and that in Paul's thought Christians are both justified by faith (*ie* restored to fellowship, acquitted), and also righteous by faith (*ie* leading a new life in Christ). These two are not identical, yet they are complementary and inseparable.

He shows that the Catholic approach to these questions has tended to regard the meaning of the noun ('righteousness') as fundamental, therefore interpreting the verb in terms of the noun, whereas Protestants have tended to do the opposite, rendering the noun as 'justification' by analogy with the meaning of the verb.

Ziesler also criticizes the traditional Protestant interpretation for over-emphasizing the alleged forensic background of this vocabulary. In his later textbook (1990, p 88), he explains that even if a legal background is pressed, the legal system in question was less concerned to pronounce innocent or guilty than to put wrongs right and to restore people to their proper place, no more and no less, in the covenant community. Justification in Paul is thus the act of restoring people to their proper relationship with God. It comes close to forgiveness, with which it is indeed equated in Rom 4.6–8.

Paul uses the word *dikaiosyne* in an unmistakably ethical sense four times in Romans 6.15–20, where sin and righteousness (*dikaiosyne*) are personified, as alternative authority-figures to whom someone might be enslaved and Christians are described as those who—having been set free from their former slavery to sin—have become slaves to righteousness (or to obedience [verse 16] or to God [verse 22]). The basis of Paul's ethical appeal here is again the 'imperative in the indicative'—since, by the grace of God, Paul's readers have transferred their allegiance from sin to righteousness, they must live righteous lives.

A similar argument occurs in 1 Corinthians 6.9–11, where Paul criticizes some of his readers for their unrighteous behaviour. He argues that their actions are fundamentally inconsistent with their Christian experience, since they have been 'washed,' 'sanctified' and 'justified.'

The occurrence of the verb 'were sanctified' in this verse alongside 'were justified' raises questions about the interpretation of Paul's concept of sanctification and its relationship to justification. The abstract nouns 'sanctification' and 'righteousness' occur in similar proximity in Romans 6.19, 22.

The concrete noun cognate with 'sanctified' and 'sanctification' is 'saint(s),' the word Paul often uses to address his readers (see Romans 1.7, 1 Corinthians 1.2, 2 Corinthians 1.1 and Philippians 1.1). In English the intrinsic connection between the noun 'saint' and the adjective 'holy' is obscured, as the two words are drawn from different roots, but in Greek the same word, *hagios*, is used for both noun and adjective.

Paul's understanding of sanctification and of holiness (drawn from his Jewish background) includes the pattern of the 'imperative in the indicative,' because the fundamental meaning of holiness is a relationship to God. In the Old Testament, 'holy' meant concerned with the service of God; the ethical sense is secondary. So the Good News Bible succeeds in conveying the basic meaning of *hagioi*, 'saints,' when it renders it as 'God's people' (2 Corinthians 1.1, Philippians 1.1) or 'God's holy people' (1 Corinthians 1.2). And 'consecration' may be a more accurate translation of *hagiasmos* than 'sanctification.'

The moral dimension of sanctification occurs most prominently in 1 Thessalonians 4, where the word occurs three times. In verse 3, *hagiasmos* is explained as 'that you avoid unchastity'; in verse 4 Paul exhorts his readers to possess their 'vessels' in *hagiasmos* and honour; and in verse 7 *hagiasmos* is contrasted with 'impurity.'

Another metaphor which Paul uses to describe what God has done in Christ for the believer is redemption. Whether he draws this image from the manumission of slaves or from the ransoming of prisoners of war, it signifies the attainment of freedom at a price. In 1 Corinthians 6.19, 20, Paul makes it clear that redemption creates a moral obligation:

You are not your own: you were bought for a price. So glorify God in your body.

The Believer's Freedom from the Law through Christ

One of the main things from which Paul claims believers have been set free by the work of Christ is the (Old Testament) Law. This is a particularly prominent theme in the epistle to the Galatians, where Paul claims that his opponents are (explicitly or implicitly) trying to reimpose the Old Testament Law as the basis of Christian identity and behaviour.

In Galatians 3.24, he uses a vivid image to describe the role of the Law, comparing it with the role of a *paidagōgos*, the slave entrusted with the care, instruction and discipline of children in a wealthy Roman household. While the heir of the household was a child, he was under the authority of the *paidagōgos*, who would treat him as he thought fit, including the imposition of corporal punishment. As soon as the young man came of age, however, he became free of the authority of the *paidagōgos*, and if he chose could even wreak revenge on him, since the *paidagōgos* was, all along, only a slave. According to this argument, the Old Testament Law was given temporary authority over the freeborn children of the household until they became mature enough to exercise their freedom responsibly; now that the children have attained adult status, they are no longer subject to the Law.

A major subject of disagreement among theologians is in what sense—according to Paul—are Christians are freed from the demands of the Law. A related question is what Paul means by his assertion in Romans 10.4 that 'Christ is the end of the Law.' One factor which has led to this important division of opinion is the wide range of meanings which the Greek word *nomos* can bear, including 'principle' and 'ruling influence' as well as 'law' in general, the 'Old Testament law' in particular, and the 'Old Testament' as a whole.

Some interpreters say that Paul believes the Law is abolished only as a way of achieving salvation. This, however, is unlikely as now it is widely acknowledged (under the influence of E P Sanders) that first-century Judaism did not inculcate salvation by obedience to the Law. So Paul's rejection of the Law is likely to have been more thorough-going.

At the opposite extreme, some readers have opted for a maximizing interpretation, sweeping away all moral restraints and claiming freedom to behave however they like. Paul, however, is at pains to make it clear that whatever he means by claiming to have been set free from the Law, he does not mean he is lawless, and in 1 Corinthians 9.21 he coins the phrase *ennomos Christou*—'under the Law of Christ'—to describe his position. The most persuasive interpretation, therefore, is that Paul believes the behaviour and standards expected of God's people (as reflected in the Old Testament Law) are unchanged, but God has established a radically new way of achieving them.

Paul sometimes describes the status and experience of believers as having been crucified and raised with Christ. The ethical implications of this doctrine are expounded at length in Romans chapter 6. In verse 6, he moves from claiming simply that 'we' have died with Christ and been buried with him through baptism, to explaining more precisely that 'our old self' (literally 'our old man') was crucified with Christ. The ethical exhortation which follows on from this theological assertion is that Paul's readers should 'consider' themselves 'to be dead to sin but alive to God in Christ Jesus.'

In Galatians 5.24, it is the *sarx* which is described as having been crucified. English translations vary considerably in how they render this Greek word. The Authorized Version, Revised Standard Version and New Revised Standard Version translate it literally, as 'flesh,' but that rendition can easily mislead readers into imagining that Paul is differentiating between physical and spiritual realms, and that he regards material reality as inherently sinful, which he certainly does not. For this reason, most modern translations have sought to convey the Apostle's meaning by rendering the word in different ways.

For example, the New International Version has translated *sarx* as 'sinful nature,' while the Revised English Bible has rendered it as 'unspiritual nature.' Both these renditions succeed in conveying the central point that *sarx* is that principle of human nature which resists the influence of the Spirit.

What God Does for the Believer through the Spirit

The objective work of God in Christ for the salvation of the world is central to Paul's message, but he is also very aware of the subjective aspect of God's saving work, performed constantly in the life of the believer by the Holy Spirit. The inter-relationship between the work of Christ and of the Spirit is expressed (although not explained) in Romans 8.2:

> The law of the Spirit of life in Christ Jesus has freed you from the law of sin and of death.

Both occurrences of the word 'law' in this verse are unclear and disputed, probably because Paul is deliberately exploiting the ambiguity of the word. Either occurrence or both could refer to the Old Testament Law or intend the word in a more general sense.

One of the principal roles of the Holy Spirit, according to Paul, is to enable believers to grow in practical holiness. He sometimes contrasts ethics based on the Spirit with ethics based on the Jewish Law. The Law seeks to steer people into right behaviour by identifying and prohibiting all other options, but the Spirit works from within, influencing desires and motives. This is what Paul has in mind in Romans 8.4, when he explains that the purpose of God's saving work in Christ was

> in order that the righteous requirement of the Law might be fulfilled in us, who walk not according to the *sarx* but according to the Spirit.

He contrasts life influenced by the *sarx* and life controlled by the Spirit, affirming in verse 9 that his readers 'are not in the *sarx* but in the Spirit.' This statement constitutes the 'indicative' which is the ground for the unfinished ethical imperative in verse 12:

> Therefore, brothers and sisters, we are under an obligation, not to the *sarx*, to live according to the *sarx*.

The other chapter in which Paul pursues a very similar train of thought is Galatians chapter 5. The motif of the 'imperative in the indicative' as regards the *sarx* and the Spirit appears more clearly in verse 25:

> If we live by the Spirit, let us walk by the Spirit.

In this chapter, Paul shows himself aware of the ambiguity of the moral and spiritual life, stating in verse 17 that there is an ethical conflict within believers between the Spirit and the *sarx*.

In Galatians 5.22–23, certain desirable moral qualities are described as constituting 'the fruit of the Spirit.' Paul's choice of this metaphor implies that the attitudes and behaviour he expects of his readers are the result of divine influence, the working of the Holy Spirit in the life of the Christian.

Implications of Belonging to God's People

Another important aspect of the 'indicative' in Paul's thinking is that believers have become incorporated into the church. This, too, has ethical implications, one of which is that natural human differences have been erased—or at least are unimportant. In 1 Corinthians 12.13 and Galatians 3.28 he explains that baptism into a single body implies that the differences between Jew and Gentile and between slave and free have ceased to be significant, and in the latter verse he adds 'male and female' to the categories superseded in Christ. An example of the practical implications is Galatians 2 where Paul describes how he condemned Peter for breaking table fellowship between Jewish and Gentile Christians.

Another ethical implication of participation in the church is that members should care for one another, especially for the edification of their fellow-believers. In 1 Corinthians 8.9–13 and 10.23, 24, this is the motive to which Paul appeals in addressing the question whether Christians should or should not eat meat which had or might have been sacrificed to pagan idols. If the exercise of Christians' liberty of action might encourage other people to contravene their own conscience, Paul argues, then they should refrain from exercising that liberty. A similar argument occurs in Romans 14.

The virtues which Paul most often describes and commends are the community virtues, those qualities—like love, forbearance and patience—which enable people to rub along together. Conversely, the 'works of the flesh' which he identifies in Galatians 5.19–21 are the vices of disunity.

Eschatology

The peculiar eschatological position of the Christian, according to Paul, has often been expressed as lying 'between the already and the not yet.' More accurately, as Hays (1996, p 21) explains,

> Paul thinks of the present time as an anomalous interval in which the 'already' and the 'not yet' of redemption exist simultaneously in dialectical tension. The ends of the ages have overlapped.

Paul's eschatological convictions have influenced his ethical teaching in three main ways. First, from the perspective of realized eschatology, certain kinds of behaviour may be considered appropriate for those who have 'already' entered the new age. Second, Paul may have believed that he would live to see Jesus come again, and that it was therefore unnecessary to develop longterm ethical strategies or codes. And third, despite Paul's constant insistence that salvation is by grace, not on the basis of good deeds, he sometimes uses the fact of future judgment as a motive for ethical behaviour.

One image which is used to express the 'already'—that of 'the Day'—has clear ethical implications. In 1 Thessalonians 5.4–8 and Romans 13.11–13, Paul exploits the ambiguity of the word 'day,' which may refer to the coming 'Day of the Lord' or to daylight by contrast with night. Although the Day of the Lord still lies in the future, Christians already 'belong to the day' (1 Thessalonians 4.8). He points out that people tend to seek the cover of darkness for the kind of behaviour of which they are or should be ashamed, but because Christians 'belong to the day,' their behaviour should be fit to be seen.

It has often been alleged that Paul, like other writers of the New Testament and perhaps even Jesus himself, believed that the Parousia—the second coming of Jesus—was imminent, and that this erroneous belief profoundly influenced his ethical teaching. One place where this theological substructure may come to the surface is 1 Corinthians 7.25–31, in which Paul's teaching about marriage is explicitly influenced by his belief that 'the appointed time has grown short' (verse 29) and that in view of 'the present necessity' (verse 26) or 'the impending distress' it may be advisable for unmarried Christians not to marry.

Those interpreters who explain 'present' as meaning 'imminent' think Paul is referring to the 'eschatological woes' which were believed would accompany the coming of the Messiah, and that he expected them to come soon. Even the literal translation 'present' is compatible with this interpretation, since Paul may be suggesting that a particular problem which his readers were then experiencing was part of the eschatological woes and thereby a sign that the Parousia would not be long delayed. Another possible interpretation, equally dependent on the belief that the Parousia was imminent, is that in Paul's mind the 'present necessity' was the urgent obligation to spread the gospel to as many people as possible during the short time that remained.

Hays (1997, p 133) points out the consequences of the intrinsic connection between eschatology and ethics in this chapter:

> The most problematical aspect of Paul's counsel on sex and marriage is that it presupposes a version of the world-story in which Paul's generation expected to see the coming of the day of the Lord. Living in the same story more than nineteen hundred years later, we know that Paul's expectation of the imminent *parousia* was wrong. Now what?

Hays's reply to his own question is

> that some rethinking and re-narration of the story is necessary. If Paul had known certainly that all of the 'virgins' whom he was advising would go to their graves without witnessing the coming of the Lord, would he so strongly have advised them to remain as they were? He does, after all, describe his opinion on this subject as precisely that: his opinion, rather than revealed knowledge. This chapter, perhaps more than any other in the New Testament, actively *invites* us into the process of rethinking and moral deliberation.

It is, however, possible to avoid this problem—as Fee (1989) does, for example—by denying that Paul's argument here was based on a belief that the Parousia was imminent. The 'present distress' could refer to some problem which Paul happened to know was afflicting his readers at the time when he wrote (such as the death of some of their members), or he could mean that—even if Jesus is not returning soon—life will be hard until he does.

The most general connection which Paul draws between the Parousia and ethics is that Christians should be blameless to meet Jesus when he comes. This thought occurs in two places in 1 Thessalonians (3.13 and 5.23); admittedly, in both places Paul is asking God to keep his readers blameless, rather than putting the onus explicitly on them, but the hint as to how they should behave is unmistakable.

In the major epistles, Paul sometimes appeals explicitly to the coming judgment as a motive for ethical behaviour. The clearest example of this motif occurs in 2 Corinthians 5.10, where—speaking of the efforts he devotes to his own ministry—he reminds his readers,

> we must all appear before the judgment seat of Christ, in order that all may receive either good or evil, according to what they have done in the body.

In 1 Corinthians 3.13–15, he compares Christian ministry with the work of a builder, building with superior or inferior materials on one foundation. He explains that each person's work will be 'revealed,' and those whose work survives being tested by fire will be rewarded, while those whose work is destroyed by the fire will barely be saved.

The theme of judgment, however, is not prominent in Paul's writings, and he is especially reluctant to use it as a threat in order to enforce good behaviour. He much prefers to emphasize positive motivation, leaving the fact of judgment in the background. In 1 Corinthians 6. 9–11, for example, he leaves his readers in no doubt of the fate naturally awaiting those who lead immoral lives, but he lays the emphasis on new life in Christ and its ethical implications:

> Those are what some of you were, but you were washed, you were sanctified, you were justified in the name of the Lord Jesus Christ, and in the Spirit of our God.

3
Sources, Methods and Guiding Principles

The Old Testament

In view of the contrast which Paul draws between Law and grace, Law and the Spirit and Law and love, it is not surprising that many commentators deny that he uses the Old Testament as a source for ethical guidance. Rosner (1995) reprints an article by Adolf Harnack (originally published in 1928) which expresses this view in forthright terms.

The alternative view is that Paul rejected the Law only as a way of salvation, and that he accepted it as binding for ethical guidance. Indeed, he states the continuing value of the Old Testament, for example Romans 15.4,

> Whatever was written in the past was written for our instruction, that through patience and the encouragement of the Scriptures we might have hope.

In 1 Corinthians 9.8–10, Paul uses Deuteronomic legislation on the treatment of domestic animals to support his claim that apostles are entitled to financial support from the churches in which they work. In the following chapter he bases strong ethical exhortations on a brief summary of the experiences of the people of Israel during their wanderings in the wilderness. He concludes (verse 11),

> These things happened to them as examples, and were written down for our admonition.

Some scholars have claimed that Paul is more heavily dependent on the Old Testament for his ethical teaching than the number of explicit quotations would suggest. On the basis of his own doctoral research, for example, Rosner (1995, p 8) argues,

> To answer Harnack on a specific example, the major lines of Paul's ethics in 1 Corinthians 5–7, a passage he describes as having hardly any links with the Old Testament (presumably because there is only one explicit citation), can be reliably traced back into the Scriptures, in many cases by way of Jewish sources.

This argument reveals that the difference in interpretation is probably not substantial. Both sides agree that Paul quite often draws on familiar ethical maxims, many of which were in fact derived from the Old Testament. But whereas some writers emphasize the origin of those precepts, others suggest that Paul may not have been conscious of their source when he used them. It is clear, however, that he does not often refer explicitly to the Old Testament for guidance or support on ethical questions, even though he discusses many subjects (such as circumcision, the Sabbath, food laws and even incest) on which it would have had insights to offer.

Current Conventions and Moral Intuitions

Paul seems to draw frequently on the conventions and moral intuitions of his Jewish and Hellenistic backgrounds for his ethical reasoning. As Houlden (1973, p 34) has well expressed it,

> as Paul's ethics spread out towards the edges, especially when he turns to questions on which it would be hard to see the bearing of central beliefs and where perhaps the best a man can do is to rationalize his prejudices or intuitive convictions, he makes use of principles which are not easily worked into the central logic of his teaching.

An example of this kind of reasoning occurs in the first part of 1 Corinthians 11, where Paul gives instructions on how women should be dressed in church. Modern commentators, such as Hays (1997, pp 182–190), find little difficulty in articulating a convincing argument in favour of Paul's injunction to Christian women to cover their heads. As in the case of food sacrificed to idols, they suggest that he may be urging Christians to restrict their freedom for the sake of other believers and the reputation of the church, since appearing in public with loose or uncovered hair was a mark of an immoral woman. But Paul himself does not use that argument, preferring to appeal to what Ziesler (1990, p 112) calls 'common decency.' His appeal to intuition is clear:

> Judge for yourselves: is it fitting for a woman to pray to God uncovered? Does not nature itself teach you…

Modern readers, however, tend to recognize that intuitions of this kind—and especially this example—are culturally based. Some have suggested that the best way for late twentieth-century readers to make use of those parts of Paul's teaching is not to follow them literally, but to translate them in terms of their own cultural background. Such a policy, however, would fail to provide a basis for a Christian critique of one's own culture. Alternatively, it can be argued that by drawing on the moral principles and standards which he had been taught, Paul endorsed them, and that he did so because he was confident that they represented the will of God.

Teaching of Jesus

There are not many occasions when Paul can appeal to the tradition of Jesus' own words to settle an ethical dilemma, but two such opportunities occur in 1 Corinthians 7.10 and 9.14. Remarkably, in the second case, he refers to Jesus' teaching, but goes on to explain that he does not obey it. In the first, Paul differentiates between those cases directly covered by the teaching of Jesus and those in which he gives guidance on a wider range of questions. The implication of verse 25 is that he prefers to appeal to a 'command of the Lord' and works out his own answer only when such a direct ruling is not available.

Other places in Paul's writings may allude indirectly to teaching attributed to Jesus in the Gospels. For example, it is possible that Romans 13.10 is a deliberate echo of Matthew 5.17, although the fact that the two verses appear to adopt such different attitudes towards the Old Testament Law, and to use the verb 'fulfil' in such different senses, counts against this hypothesis.

The Mind of Christ and the Guidance of the Spirit

At the end of 1 Corinthians 7, having carefully differentiated between the teaching of Jesus and his own opinion, Paul substantiates his right to express his opinion in this way by saying 'And I think I, too, have the Spirit of God.' A similar expression occurs in 1 Corinthians 2.16, although not in an explicitly ethical context, when Paul says that he and his readers 'have the mind of Christ.' The potential of this concept for ethics is highlighted in Romans 12.2, where Paul urges his readers, as their response to the gospel,

> Do not be conformed to this age, but be transformed by the renewal of your mind, that you may test what is the will of God, what is good and pleasing and perfect.

These quotations can be interpreted as hinting at a different approach to ethics, which some ethicists of our own day find congenial, namely, looking to the Bible and the Christian faith not for answers to ethical dilemmas but for ethical and spiritual formation. As Stanley Hauerwas and others have argued, Christian ethics is inseparable from Christian discipleship, which is in turn based on and influenced by the constant reiteration of the Christian story.

Love

I have already pointed out the connection between love as a guiding principle and participation in the church as a source of ethical motivation. This connection is the basis of the best-known description of love, 1 Corinthians 13, which is set in the context of a discussion of spiritual gifts. In chapters 12 and 14, the apostle urges his readers to respect one another, especially those whose gifts and roles are relatively unspectacular, and urges them to value most the gifts which build up the church. In chapter 13, Paul points out 'an even better way,' explaining that the work of the Spirit which should impress his readers most is love. The central section of this 'hymn to love' (verses 4–7) describes the practical outworkings of love, which are the virtues of community life.

Paul's theory of love in Christian ethics resembles his understanding of the work of the Spirit in ethics. The behaviour which is prompted from within by love is the very same as that which the Law had vainly tried to impose from without; in short (Romans 13.10), 'love does no evil to a neighbour; therefore love is the fulfilment of the Law.'

This insight is the culmination of an argument in which Paul claims (verse 9) that the laws in the second half of the Ten Commandments can be 'summed up in this word, namely "Love your neighbour as yourself." ' He makes the same point in slightly different words in Galatians 5.14.

Imitation of Christ

The most powerful example of Paul's ethical appeal to the imitation of Christ occurs in Philippians 2.1–11, where a theological description of the story of Jesus is used as the basis of a call for unity in the church. Paul appeals to the Incarnation as an example of humility, self-denial and concern for others. He argues in a similar way in Romans 15.2–4, while in 2 Corinthians 8.9 he appeals to the generosity of Jesus as a motive for generous giving.

Paul quite often refers to the example of his own attitudes and behaviour, and in 1 Thessalonians 1.6 and 1 Corinthians 1.11 he is so confident of his own success in following Jesus' example that he can advise his readers that one way of imitating Jesus is to imitate him.

Principles in Action

Richard Hays (1996, p 43) well describes Paul's ethical methods in action, in relation to the issue at Corinth of eating meat which had, or might have been, sacrificed to idols:

> Paul addresses this pastoral problem at Corinth not by seeking to determine the appropriate *halakah* in the Torah, not by pointing to the authoritative teaching of Jesus or the pronouncement of an Apostolic Council (Acts 15) but by urging the strong members of the Corinthian church to follow the example of Christ and the example of the apostle by surrendering their place of privilege. The *telos* of such action is not just to enhance personal virtue and humility but also to secure the unity of the community in Christ. The ethical norm, then, is not given in the form of a predetermined rule or set of rules for conduct; rather, the right action must be *discerned* on the basis of a christological paradigm, with a view to the need of the community.

4
Teaching on Specific Subjects

Sex and Marriage

1 Corinthians 7 is the only place where Paul devotes more than a passing reference to sex and marriage. Commentators generally agree that his opening words—'It is good for a man not to touch a woman'—are a quotation or paraphrase from the reported views of the Corinthians, not Paul's own teaching. It appears that some Corinthians taught that Christian couples who aspired to true holiness should abstain from sexual relations. In response, Paul states that husbands and wives have authority over one another's bodies, and he urges that they give each other what they owe. He allows that a couple might abstain from sex in order to devote themselves to prayer, but only if both agree and only for a limited period; he makes it clear that this is a concession, not a recommendation.

Paul's advice to unmarried Christians is that there are advantages in remaining single, but it would not be a sin for them to marry. Some modern interpreters think that because the conditions which caused Paul to be so aware of the advantages of the single state no longer apply, the balance between marriage and singleness should therefore be struck in a somewhat different place.

Paul's attitude to divorce is similar to that found in the gospels, although it differs from them in detail. Both approaches combine opposition to divorce in principle with a pragmatic and humane recognition of the needs of actual situations. Reading between the lines of 1 Corinthians 7, it appears that some Corinthian Christians were deserting their partners and forming new relationships on rather flimsy grounds, either on the basis that because they were new creatures in Christ, their marriage relationships had been superseded and they were free to marry again 'in the Lord,' or under pressure from the church to avoid being polluted by an intimate relationship with an unconverted spouse.

Paul's advice is that his readers should preserve their marriages if at all possible but should not feel bound to a spouse who insists on divorce. One can interpret the New Testament teaching on divorce strictly, allowing it only under the conditions specifically identified in 1 Corinthians and Matthew, or one can argue that both Paul and the gospels allow for the possibility of divorce in hard cases of various kinds while at the same time urging that no one should resort to it lightly.

Money and Possessions

As in his discussion of other subjects, Paul urges his readers to treat money and possessions in the light of their eschatological provisionality; in 1 Corinthians 7.30, 31, for example:

let those who buy do so as those who do not possess anything, and those who use the world do so as those who do not make full use of it, for the form of this world is passing away.

Apart from that basic perception, the main two themes of his teaching on these subjects are honesty and generosity. There are brief exhortations against covetousness and dishonesty in 1 Corinthians 5.10 and 6.10, but the focus of Paul's most extensive teaching about money and possessions concerns the collection for the poor Christians in Jerusalem, which he mentions briefly in Romans 15.26–27 and Galatians 2.10 and discusses at length in 2 Corinthians 8 and 9, which many interpreters think were originally separate from one another and from the epistle. In those two chapters, Paul refers to several motives for generosity, some theological (8.9, 9.8–11), some psychological (8.8, 9.2–4) and some apparently based on self-interest (8.14, 9.6). He articulates some memorable principles, such as 'God loves a cheerful giver' (9.7) and gives practical advice on how this generosity is to be managed.

The State

The main passage in which Paul discusses the attitude of Christians to the state is Romans 13.1–7, where he urges his readers to 'submit to the ruling authorities' (verse 1) who 'have been instituted by God' (verse 1) and 'are God's servants' (verses 6, 4). Many commentators have been surprised by the positive attitude towards the state, especially since the emperor at the time was Nero. Others have speculated that Paul may have changed his attitude later, but if he did, he left no trace of it.

By contrast, Paul's descriptions in 2 Corinthians 6.5 and 11.23–25, 32–33 of his own experiences at the hands of the authorities show that—despite the conservatism of Romans 13.1–7—his principles and actions frequently brought him into conflict with Jewish and Roman authorities and also that he had no illusions about the use and abuse of power.

There is an obvious difference of tone between Romans 13.1–7 and 1 Corinthians 6.1–8, where Paul criticizes Christians who resort to the pagan courts in order to settle their differences. Recent sociological studies have revealed that civil cases under Roman law in general, and in Corinth in particular, were usually brought by the rich and powerful against the poor and weak, and that the rich generally won. So when Paul describes judges as 'unjust' or 'unrighteous,' he may well mean both that they are outside God's covenant people and that they are biassed in favour of their friends. At the least, Paul protests, Christians who cannot agree over some issue should refer it to a tribunal drawn from the church itself, but preferably should act generously towards one another and refrain from insisting on their own rights. Despite the harsh words which Paul applies to the legal system, Schrage (1988, p 239) rightly points out that he does not deny in principle the power and right of the state to decide civil cases any more than he denies the state's general purpose of maintaining order and justice. He makes it abundantly clear, however, that the function of the state and its legal system do not in themselves necessarily serve the ends of the gospel and love, not even when the state is carrying out its legitimate mission.

Slavery

People who argue that the influence of Christianity in the world has been largely beneficial often point out that the abolition of slavery in the British Empire was achieved through the efforts of devout Christians whose arguments were explicitly biblical and theological. True though this is, they less often admit that the opponents of emancipation were equally devout Christians, whose arguments were no less biblical or theological. Excluding the exhortations to masters and slaves in the 'household codes' in Colossians, Ephesians and 1 Peter, the sources for identifying Paul's attitude to slavery are the epistle to Philemon and 1 Corinthians chapter 7.

More than any other letter attributed to Paul, the epistle to Philemon is a personal letter to an individual and is not intended for a church. The three characters in the story which lies behind the epistle are Paul, Philemon and Onesimus, who is apparently Philemon's slave. Onesimus has wronged Philemon in some way (probably by running away), but he has subsequently become a Christian through Paul's ministry. Paul's purpose in writing the letter is to intercede for Onesimus, reminding Philemon that he, too, came to faith through his ministry.

It is unclear precisely what Paul is asking Philemon to do. In particular, commentators vary as to whether he expects him to free Onesimus from slavery or not. In verses 15, 16, Paul envisages that Philemon will

> have [Onesimus] back for ever, no longer as a slave, but more than a slave, a beloved brother…

He then urges Philemon to receive Onesimus as he would receive Paul himself and offers to repay whatever Onesimus owes, but then makes it clear that he does not expect his offer to be accepted. Finally, in verse 21 he expresses his confidence that Philemon will do more than he has asked of him. Barclay depicts the difficulties which would be caused to Philemon and other moderately wealthy Christians if they were expected either to free slaves who became Christians or to treat their Christian slaves as brothers. He suggests (p 117)

> that the ambiguities we have noted in the letter to Philemon reflect the difficulties in finding any clear solution to this problem. It is arguable that the tortured 'no longer as a slave but as more than a slave, a beloved brother'

indicates Paul's struggle with this problem, in the awareness that the master-slave relationship was impossible to square with that of brother to brother; but the lack of a clear recommendation for manumission may represent his awareness of the difficulties Philemon, and other church hosts, would face in this regard.

There is even less support for a radical critique of slavery in 1 Corinthians 7.20–24, where Paul uses slavery as an example of the principle that Christians should remain in the situation in which they were called:

> Were you called as a slave? Do not let it bother you. If you can become free, make use of it. For anyone who was called in the Lord as a slave is the freedman of the Lord; likewise, anyone who was called as a free person is the slave of Christ.

To make Paul's attitude to this subject even more problematic, the third sentence in this quotation is ambiguous. He may mean either 'But if you have an opportunity to gain your freedom, take advantage of it' or, 'Even if you do have an opportunity to gain your freedom, rather make use of your status as a slave.' The former is more probable.

Barclay (1997) shows how some exegetes have claimed that by not opposing the institution of slavery, Paul implicitly supported it, whereas others have discerned in his comments on the subject the seeds of the later abolition movement—even though it took nearly two thousand years to bear fruit. He concludes (p 125) by regretting

> Paul's inability (or unwillingness) to encourage, or even to conceive, different forms of social interdependence, even within the church. Here indeed much hinges on one's understanding of the Christian gospel: is it confined to individual salvation and 'spiritual truths,' or has it the power to critique contemporary social practices and the fertility to spawn fresh alternatives?

5
Conclusion

Of the three elements in Paul's ethical teaching which I have identified, he deals most fully and most clearly with the first, 'ethical motivation.' This dimension of Paul's ethical teaching is most fundamental to his overall message and poses fewest hermeneutical difficulties. He expounds the gospel in various ways which make its ethical implications unmistakably clear, asking for example, 'We died to sin: so how can we still live in it?' (Romans 6.2). He does this partly in order to defend himself against allegations of antinomianism and partly in response to particular problems which had occurred in the churches to which he writes.

When discussing particular ethical issues, Paul draws on various sources and appeals to several guiding principles. In some cases, there is room for disagreement as to whether the methods or the contents are more important for those seeking to appropriate his teaching. At present, this uncertainty is particularly relevant to relations between the sexes. Should Christian women wear hats (or veils) in church (1 Corinthians 11:5), and should they "keep silent" (1 Corinthians 14:34)? Because Paul himself gives few clues as to how culture-specific this teaching is, different readers will inevitably interpret it in different ways. Similarly, when Paul cites homosexual acts as an example of sinful behaviour (in Romans 1.26, 27 and 1 Corinthians 6.9), is he passing an inspired and authoritative judgment, or is he merely taking for granted the prejudices of his own background? Although opinions can legitimately differ, there can be little doubt that the great principles to which he appeals—especially love and the example of Christ—should be central to a Christian approach to ethical issues.

As my summaries of Paul's views on particular subjects has shown, he is less comprehensive, less radical and more ambiguous than some would wish. Barclay (1997, p 125) forcefully expresses the challenge to Paul's conservatism:

> For many Christians, the credibility of their faith is at stake in the question whether Philemon, or the New Testament, or the Christian tradition generally, contains the resources which enable the church to critique the distorted ideologies and social injustices of our contemporary society, even if those resources have to be, quite explicitly, developed well beyond their original range.

Some would argue that an appropriate way of putting Paul's teaching into practice today is to use his methods in new contexts, and even to draw out some implications of his teaching which he may not have recognized himself. The practical end results of such reasoning may be very different from Paul's own concrete ethical exhortations and judgments.

6
References and Recommended Reading

Barclay, John M G, 1988, *Obeying the Truth: A Study of Paul's Ethics in Galatians* (Edinburgh: T & T Clark).

Barclay, John M G, 1997, *Colossians and Philemon (New Testament Guides)* (Sheffield: Sheffield Academic Press).

Cranfield, C E B, 1975/1979, *A Critical and Exegetical Commentary on the Epistle to the Romans (International Critical Commentary)* (Edinburgh: T & T Clark).

Dunn, James D G, 1988, *Romans (Word Biblical Commentary)* (Dallas: Word).

Fee, Gordon D, 1987, *The First Epistle to the Corinthians (New International Commentary on the New Testament)* (Grand Rapids: Eerdmans).

Frör, Hans, 1995, *You Wretched Corinthians! The Correspondence Between the Church in Corinth and Paul* (London: SCM).

Furnish, Victor P, 1968, *Theology and Ethics in Paul* (Nashville: Abingdon).

Hays, Richard B, 1996, *The Moral Vision of the New Testament: A Contemporary Introduction to New Testament Ethics* (Edinburgh: T & T Clark).

Hays, Richard B, 1997, *First Corinthians (Interpretation: A Bible Commentary for Teaching and Preaching)* (Louisville: John Knox).

Houlden, J L, 1973, *Ethics and the New Testament* (Harmondsworth: Penguin).

Hurd, J C, 1983, *The Origin of 1 Corinthians* (Macon, Georgia: Mercer University Press, New Edition).

Matera, Frank J, 1996, *New Testament Ethics: The Legacies of Jesus and Paul* (Louisville, Kentucky: Westminster John Knox, part 4)

Moo, Douglas, 1996, *The Epistle to the Romans (New International Commentary)* (Grand Rapids: Eerdmans).

Rosner, Brian S (ed), 1995, *Understanding Paul's Ethics: Twentieth-Century Approaches* (Carlisle: Paternoster).

Schrage, W, 1988, *The Ethics of the New Testament* (Edinburgh: T & T Clark, chapter 4).

Ziesler, John A, 1972, *The Meaning of Righteousness in Paul* (Cambridge: Cambridge University Press).

Ziesler, John A, 1990, *Pauline Christianity* (Oxford: Oxford University Press, Revised Edition).

Ziesler, John A, 1989, *Paul's Letter to the Romans (TPI New Testament Commentaries)* (London: SCM).